DIMENSIONS OF HEALTH

EMOTIONAL HEALTH

by Kelsey Jopp

FOCUS READERS
NAVIGATOR

WWW.FOCUSREADERS.COM

Copyright © 2026 by Focus Readers®, Mendota Heights, MN 55120. All rights reserved. No part of this book may be reproduced or utilized in any form or by any means without written permission from the publisher.

Focus Readers is distributed by North Star Editions:
sales@northstareditions.com | 888-417-0195

Produced for Focus Readers by Red Line Editorial.

Photographs ©: iStockphoto, cover, 1, 11; Shutterstock Images, 4–5, 7, 8–9, 12, 15, 16–17, 20–21, 23, 25, 26–27, 29; Red Line Editorial, 18

Library of Congress Cataloging-in-Publication Data
Library of Congress Cataloging-in-Publication Data is available on the Library of Congress website.

ISBN
979-8-88998-524-2 (hardcover)
979-8-88998-584-6 (ebook pdf)
979-8-88998-556-3 (hosted ebook)

Printed in the United States of America
Mankato, MN
082025

ABOUT THE AUTHOR
Kelsey Jopp is a writer, counselor, and lifelong learner. She lives in Minnesota, where she enjoys swimming in lakes and playing with her labradoodle, Rudy.

TABLE OF CONTENTS

CHAPTER 1
A Tough Day 5

CHAPTER 2
What Is Emotional Health? 9

CONNECTIONS
Emotional and Social Health 14

CHAPTER 3
Understanding Emotions 17

CHAPTER 4
Planning and Practice 21

CHAPTER 5
Taking Care 27

Focus Questions • 30
Glossary • 31
To Learn More • 32
Index • 32

CHAPTER 1

A TOUGH DAY

A girl is having a terrible day. First, she was late to school. Then she realized she forgot her art project at home. In gym class, she got hit by a basketball. All she wants to do is go home and read.

However, when she gets home, the girl can't find her book. She calls out to ask if her dad has seen it, but he is upstairs

> Facing problems can bring up feelings of anger or sadness.

and can't hear her. The girl stomps up the stairs. She wants to yell. Instead, she slowly counts to 10. She reminds herself that it's not her dad's fault she is having a bad day.

The girl's dad sees her and asks what is wrong. She takes a deep breath and tells him why she feels angry. Together, they

BREATHING DEEPLY

Calming down helps make it easier to deal with frustrating problems. Deep breathing is one way to calm down. Take a long breath in through your nose, like you're smelling a flower. Then breathe out through your mouth, like you're blowing out a candle. Repeat both steps three times.

Taking deep breaths can help people feel calmer. So can thinking of somewhere peaceful.

look for her book. They find it behind the couch. The girl still feels a bit mad. But she knows it's okay. Tomorrow will be a new day.

CHAPTER 2

WHAT IS EMOTIONAL HEALTH?

Life's joys and challenges cause people to feel many emotions. Emotional health is about how people **cope** with these feelings. It involves being able to name your feelings and **express** them in **appropriate** ways.

Some emotions, such as happiness, can feel good. Others are not so fun.

> People often feel several emotions at once. For example, they might feel both nervous and excited on the first day of school.

9

Examples include fear, anger, and sadness. People may want to avoid some feelings. However, all emotions are important. Emotionally healthy people feel a wide range of emotions. They know how to tell these feelings apart. And they know helpful ways to deal with each one.

For instance, suppose someone is sad. They might ask a friend for a hug. Or they might draw a picture showing how they feel. Both actions are healthy ways to express sadness. People don't pretend the feeling doesn't exist. Instead, they do things that help them move through it.

Some life situations make emotional health more difficult. Facing high levels

Getting outside for a walk or a run can help lift a person's mood.

of **stress** is one example. For instance, suppose a boy has just moved to a new city. He starts going to a new school. He doesn't know anyone there. The boy might feel too overwhelmed to name how he feels. But the feelings are still there.

 Having family members who fight often can be a source of stress.

And they might come out in unhealthy ways. For example, the boy might shout at his siblings or stop doing his homework.

Having unmet needs can be another challenge. Some people don't have safe places to live or enough food to eat. This causes stress. It can also spark strong emotions. When people are hungry, they may feel tired or angry more often. They may also have a hard time thinking clearly. Managing emotions in healthy ways becomes more difficult.

Emotionally healthy people still go through hard things. But they tend to be more **resilient**. They know that feelings don't last forever. And they know how to ask for help. In fact, having support is a big factor in emotional health. People with strong connections to others tend to be better at managing their feelings. They are also less at risk for anxiety or **depression**.

> CONNECTIONS

EMOTIONAL AND SOCIAL HEALTH

Emotional health and social health are closely related. Social health is the ability to make and keep healthy relationships. People in healthy relationships show care for one another. They may sometimes argue. But they can talk things through with respect. They think of how others might feel. And they stop and think before they act. They try not to do or say things that would be hurtful.

Healthy relationships improve emotional health. Friends or family can help when a person feels sad or angry. They can listen as the person talks about their feelings. They can help the person process those emotions. Sometimes, just spending time together is enough. Having fun and feeling cared about can lift a person's mood.

Friends and family can help people feel seen and cared for during hard times.

Unhealthy relationships have the opposite effect. In unhealthy relationships, people act in ways that are cruel or hurtful. This can produce several harmful results. People may feel pressure to hide their feelings. They might fear making the other person angry. Or they might copy unhealthy behaviors. They might snap back. Or they might **bully** others.

CHAPTER 3

UNDERSTANDING EMOTIONS

Emotional health often starts with understanding emotions. People feel many different emotions. Knowing words to describe them is helpful. For example, *hurt*, *lonely*, and *disappointed* all describe types of sadness. But each has a different cause. Being able to tell them apart helps people know how to respond.

▶ People can learn about their emotions by writing about how they feel.

Paying attention to what happens in the body helps, too. When someone feels scared, their heart beats faster. Their palms may get sweaty. People can learn

FEELINGS WHEEL

This chart shows a few basic emotions, as well as some more-specific forms of each one.

to recognize signs like this. That can help them name and cope with feelings.

Schools and libraries can be good places to learn more about emotions. Teachers can help answer questions. Many schools also have counselors or **psychologists**. Students can meet with them for support and advice.

FEELINGS JOURNAL

Keeping a feelings journal is one way to practice paying attention to emotions. When an emotion comes up, write it down. Write when and where it happened. At the end of the week, read through the journal. Notice which emotions came up most. If you have questions, share what you noticed with a trusted adult.

CHAPTER 4

PLANNING AND PRACTICE

Emotions can be powerful. They can feel like they will last forever. Or they might make you feel an **urge** to act right away. But to deal with emotions in healthy ways, it's important to stop and think. That lets you decide if an action would be helpful or not.

▶ When people experience big feelings, they may want to give up or shut down.

21

Good decisions are based on values. A value is a trait that someone cares about. Examples are kindness, honesty, and courage. When people experience strong emotions, they can sometimes forget their values. As a result, they may act in ways they will **regret** later. For instance, they might say something mean. Instead, people can pause and take a breath. This gives them time to remember their values. They can then choose to act in ways that match.

Planning ahead helps, too. People can set goals. They can plan ways to cope when emotions come up. For example, a girl might want to fight less often with

If people act in ways that they regret, they can say they are sorry.

her sibling. So, she might plan to go into another room when she starts to feel annoyed.

People can also pay attention to their thoughts. They can notice what they are thinking before and after a feeling comes up. They can watch for thoughts that are not true or not helpful. For instance, suppose a boy makes a mistake. He might think, *I can't do anything right.* Then he feels worse. If thoughts are causing problems, people can practice new ways of thinking. For example, the boy could tell himself, *It's normal to make mistakes.*

Changing thought patterns and behaviors can be tricky. It takes practice.

GOOD GOALS

The most-useful goals are clear and doable. If goals are not clear, people can lose focus. And if goals are too hard, people can feel stressed or give up. However, no one meets their goals all of the time. If you miss a goal, don't give up. Instead, try again.

A school counselor can help students set goals and make plans to meet them.

People may also need support. Adults often have more experience dealing with emotions. So, kids can ask teachers or family members for advice. School counselors can help make goals and plans. And therapists can teach skills for dealing with difficult thoughts or feelings.

CHAPTER 5

TAKING CARE

People make lots of decisions in a day. Many of these decisions seem small. But they add up. Together, they can have a big impact on a person's emotional health. For example, being tired can make anger or sadness harder to deal with. So, getting enough sleep is one way to help your emotional health.

Using phones or other screens right before bed can make it hard to sleep.

Exercise is important as well. Being active helps people's bodies process stress. It can also lift people's moods. Planning time for rest and hobbies helps, too. Both are good ways to calm difficult emotions.

People can also help others be healthy. They can encourage friends and family

LISTENING WELL

When someone is talking, try not to be distracted. To show you are listening, you can nod and make eye contact. You can also repeat part of what the person says. For example, you might say, "It makes sense that you're feeling sad." Or you might say, "I feel angry sometimes, too." This shows that you understand.

Friends can help each other name and process feelings.

to make good decisions. And they can provide support when people are struggling. If someone you know is going through a hard time, reach out. Ask how they are feeling. Listen carefully to their response. And encourage them to ask for help if they need it.

FOCUS QUESTIONS

Write your answers on a separate piece of paper.

1. Write a sentence that describes the main ideas of Chapter 3.

2. Do you find it easy or hard to name what you are feeling? Why do you think that is?

3. What is an example of a healthy way to express sadness?
   - A. pretending not to be sad
   - B. drawing how you feel
   - C. shouting at a friend

4. What could be a healthy response if someone is feeling angry?
   - A. slamming a door
   - B. going for a walk
   - C. shoving a person

Answer key on page 32.

GLOSSARY

appropriate
Fitting for the situation.

bully
To hurt other people and make them feel powerless.

cope
To deal with something difficult.

depression
A medical condition of deep, long-lasting sadness or loss of interest.

express
To show or tell others how one feels.

psychologists
People who are experts on the mind and how it works.

regret
To wish that something had not happened.

resilient
Able to heal and become stronger after a hard time.

stress
A feeling of tension or pressure caused by the things going on around someone.

urge
A strong desire to do a certain behavior, often right away.

TO LEARN MORE

BOOKS

Hubbard, Ben. *Less Stress: Developing Stress-Management Skills.* Capstone Press, 2021.

Kukla, Lauren. *Breathe with Art! Activities to Manage Emotions.* Abdo Publishing, 2023.

Markovics, Joyce. *Emotions.* Cherry Lake Publishing, 2022.

NOTE TO EDUCATORS

Visit **www.focusreaders.com** to find lesson plans, activities, links, and other resources related to this title.

INDEX

anger, 6, 10, 13, 14–15, 18, 27–28

behaviors, 15, 24
bodies, 18, 28

connections, 13

decisions, 21–22, 27, 29
disappointed, 17–18

exercise, 28

goals, 22, 24–25

healthy, 10, 13, 14, 21, 28

moods, 14, 28

needs, 12

psychologists, 19

relationships, 14–15

sadness, 10, 14, 17–18, 27–28

school, 5, 11, 19, 25
sleep, 27
stress, 11, 13, 24, 28
support, 13, 19, 25, 29

thoughts, 23–25

unhealthy, 12, 15

values, 22